Mark Meynell

Colossians & Philemon

Confident Christianity

GOOD BOOK GUIDE

7-Session Bible Study

Colossians and Philemon: Confident Christianity
A Good Book Guide

This edition printed 2025.

Published by The Good Book Company

thegoodbook.com | thegoodbook.co.uk
thegoodbook.com.au | thegoodbook.co.nz

A CIP catalogue record for this book is available from the British Library.

Design by André Parker and Drew McCall

ISBN: 9781802541595 | JOB-008396 | Printed in India

Contents

Introduction

One of the Bible writers described God's word as "a lamp for my feet, a light on my path" (Psalm 119:105, NIV). God gave us the Bible to tell us about who he is and what he wants for us. He speaks through it by his Spirit and lights our way through life.

That means that we need to look carefully at the Bible and uncover its meaning—but we also need to apply what we've discovered to our lives.

Good Book Guides are designed to help you do just that. The sessions in this book are interactive and easy to lead. They're perfect for use in groups or for personal study.

Let's take a look at what is included in each session.

Talkabout: Every session starts with an ice-breaker question, designed to get people talking around a subject that links to the Bible study.

Investigate: These questions help you explore what the passage is about.

Apply: These questions are designed to get you thinking practically: what does this Bible teaching mean for you and your church?

Explore More: These optional sections help you to go deeper or to explore another part of the Bible which connects with the main passage.

Getting Personal: These sections are a chance for personal reflection. Some groups may feel comfortable discussing these, but you may prefer to look at them quietly as individuals instead—or leave them out.

Pray: Here, you're invited to pray in the light of the truths and challenges you've seen in the study.

Each session is also designed to be easily split into two! Watch out for the **Apply** section that comes halfway through, and stop there if you haven't got time to do the whole thing in one go.

In the back of the book, you'll find a **Leader's Guide**, which provides helpful notes on every question, along with everything else that group leaders need in order to facilitate a great session and help the group uncover the riches of God's light-giving word.

Why Study Colossians and Philemon?

It happens all the time...

People who start out well as Christians can end up light years from the gospel of Jesus Christ, caught up in weird and not-so-wonderful cults, movements and traditions. And not just individuals but whole churches and church movements. They may still talk about Jesus, but their focus has shifted from the fundamental truths of who he is and what he has done to other things: rituals, rapturous experiences, morality or an intense engagement with ideas and schools of thought. These other things become the focus of our Christianity. It seems that Jesus Christ and his saving death are no longer enough.

This kind of teaching was the reason why Paul wrote his letter to the Colossian church. He recognised the fall-out of "moving on" from the gospel—we become unsure of God's forgiveness because it no longer depends solely on Jesus; we become proud of what we do; and ultimately, these new ways of thinking and alternative spiritualities completely fail to deliver the new life and fulfilment that they promise.

But Paul shows us not just the *better* way but the *only true way* to grow and be fruitful as a Christian believer. And it starts by understanding exactly who Jesus Christ is: the God who created and sustains the world—indeed the very reason that we exist at all. The fact that this awesome ruler of the universe became a man and died to reconcile us to God is the heart of the Christian gospel, which not only saves us but is also the only basis for genuine Christian growth.

Undoubtedly, Christians today face the same danger. These six studies can help us resist the fine-sounding arguments that entice us to add to what Jesus has already done. Only if we are convinced about the true identity of Christ, and certain that he alone is all we need to grow, will we mature into confident Christians.

The six studies in this Good Book Guide will help groups and individuals find the way to achieve true Christian growth into confidence and fruitfulness.

NOTE: With the exception of session 7, this study guide was put together using the 1984 edition of the New International Version of the Bible. Unless otherwise indicated, all Bible quotations come from that translation. Occasionally this is different from the 2011 NIV.

GOOD BOOK GUIDE — BIBLE TIMELINE

- Creation
- Fall
- Noah
- Abraham
- Joseph
- Exodus from Egypt
- Israel reaches promised land
- King David
- Kingdom divided (Judah/Israel)
- Israel exiled
- Judah exiled
- Judah returns
- Jesus Christ
- Pentecost
- Jerusalem destroyed
- Revelation written
- Now
- Jesus' return New creation

Colossians & Philemon
c. 60-61 AD

c. 54-56 Paul in Ephesus. Epaphras is converted and takes the gospel to Colossae.

c. 60-61 Paul writes Colossians, Ephesians and Philemon while under house arrest in Rome.

c. 62 Paul released.

1

Jesus Our Confidence

Colossians 1:1-14

Talkabout

1. What things do you give thanks to God for and/or pray for the most?

In his opening paragraphs, Paul tells the Colossians what is filling his prayers; and even though he has never met them, it is the Colossians themselves!

Investigate

📖 **Read Colossians 1:1-8**

DICTIONARY

Holy (v 2): set apart, pure.
Grace (v 2): undeserved kindness.
Saints (v 4): Christians. (This word literally means "distinctive people".)

Having heard news of the Colossians from their friend Epaphras (v 7, 8), Paul is greatly encouraged because all the signs point to their walk with Jesus being genuine.

2. What evidence is there for the Colossians' conversion?

3. Read verse 5. In what ways does hope motivate faith and love, do you think?

4. The New Testament describes conversion to Christ in various ways. What is unusual about Paul's description in verses 5-8?

- Why is this change not simply a matter of intellectual understanding?

📖 Read Colossians 1:9-11

Paul's prayer moves naturally from thanking God to asking God, because he recognises that Epaphras' news is just the start. What matters now is how these Colossian Christians grow to maturity. We sometimes find it difficult to pray for people that we have never met. Paul has no such trouble, and his prayer takes us to the heart of what is most important in the Christian life.

5. What does Paul specifically pray for in verse 9?

6. Why are these things important? (See verses 10-11.)

7. What is the link between knowledge and wisdom, and good works (v 9-10)?

Getting Personal | OPTIONAL

What we praise God for and pray for reveals what is most important to us. When was the last time you thanked God for the faith, love and hope of your friends and family? Or prayed for these things to grow?

Read Colossians 1:12-14

It's crucial to recognise that Paul is not expecting the Colossians to "turn over a new leaf" in their lives, as if they could suddenly decide to be good. The spiritual growth he prays for comes from a deeper appreciation of what God has already done for and in them.

8. Note the tense of these verses (past, present or future). List all the things that the Father has done. How did he achieve them?

9. So how can a Christian have confidence when faced with the challenge to endure with patience and joy? (See verse 11.)

Explore More | OPTIONAL

Read 1 Thessalonians 1:1-10

- What are the similarities and differences between Paul's prayers in this passage and the one in Colossians 1:3-14?

Apply

10. What are the challenges from this passage for our priorities in prayer?

11. What will the cost be for us, if we are to be faithful followers of Christ?

12. How can we contribute to the gospel bearing fruit? (Clue: How did it bear fruit in the Colossians' lives, according to verse 6?)

Pray

Thank God for...

- *the gospel of grace, which gives spiritual failures confidence to live for God.*
- *those you know who live a life of faith, love and hope.*
- *the fact that the gospel is still bearing fruit all over the world (and thank him for specific places you are familiar with).*

Ask God...

- *to deepen your knowledge of God's will so that you might live to please God.*
- *to bring others to hear and understand God's grace.*
- *to help you endure by his strengthening power.*

2

Jesus Our Lord

Colossians 1:15-23

The Story So Far...

Growing in the Christian life is about understanding and relying on what God has done for us in Christ.

Talkabout

1. If they give Jesus any thought at all, how do your friends and colleagues tend to view him? What relevance would they say that he has for life today?

Investigate

Read Colossians 1:15-20

DICTIONARY

Firstborn (v 15, 18): the heir, the son who will inherit.

Reconcile (v 20): bring into relationship.

2. Underline or write down each time Paul uses the words "all", "every" and "full". What point is Paul making?

3. Spot the parallels between the two halves of this passage.

	Verses 15-17 (Creation)	Verses 18-20 (Rescue)
How is Jesus described?		
What does Jesus achieve?		

- Why is it important that Jesus is God's image?

4. Reread verses 13-17. Paul makes astonishing claims about what God has done through Jesus (v 13-14). What qualifies Jesus to bring about this rescue (v 15)?

5. How does the universe depend on Jesus? Describe the past and present aspects of this relationship.

6. Why does Paul spell out that Christ's authority even extends to human rulers (v 16)? (Clue: Look at 4:18!)

Having outlined Jesus' triumph in the creation of the universe, Paul now shifts to his triumph in rescuing the universe.

7. Reread 1:18-20. Why is it important we understand that Jesus is the "head of the body, the church"?

8. What is the extent of Jesus' victory on the cross (v 20)?

- How would you explain *how* his death on the cross makes peace?

Explore More | OPTIONAL

Read John 1:1-14 and Hebrews 1:1-4

- What do these add to our understanding of Jesus' identity and mission?

Apply

9. How might you respond to a Christian friend who says, "All you need to know about Jesus is that he died to forgive us"?

10. What would you say to a friend who thinks Jesus is irrelevant?

Investigate

Read Colossians 1:21-23

DICTIONARY

Alienated (v 21): had no relationship at all.

Blemish (v 22): imperfection.

11. What has changed in the Colossians' lives, and how did that come about?

Getting Personal | OPTIONAL

What has changed in your own life since you first encountered Jesus? What steps do you need to take to remain "established and firm" in your faith?

12. What will a confident Christian look like? (See verse 23.)

Apply

13. What difficulties do you face in proclaiming the gospel to others?

- How does this passage encourage and strengthen you for that?

Pray

Thank God for...

- *the confidence of knowing Jesus' cosmic authority as Creator and Rescuer.*
- *your own reconciliation to God.*

Ask God...

- *for the ability to continue in your faith, unmoved from the gospel's hope.*
- *to change the hearts of friends who fail to recognise Jesus' authority.*

3

Jesus Our Rock

Colossians 1:24 - 2:7

The Story So Far...

Growing in the Christian life is about understanding and relying on what God has done for us in Christ.

We can be confident in Jesus because of who he is—the full image of God—and what he has done—dying to reconcile a rebellious world to God.

Talkabout

1. What things shake your confidence as a Christian?

Paul endured a great deal in his life—including insults, beatings and imprisonments—all for preaching Jesus.

Investigate

📖 **Read Colossians 1:24-29**

DICTIONARY

Afflictions (v 24): sufferings.

Commission (v 25): job, specific role.

2. What enabled Paul to persevere and even rejoice in the midst of his sufferings?

A "mystery" in the Bible is not something strange or spooky. Instead it is something that was secret but is now out in the open and is public knowledge.

3. What exactly is the "mystery" God has chosen to reveal to the Gentiles, and why is it so remarkable?

4. Spell out the part God plays in the preaching of the gospel, and the part Paul plays. What is the ultimate goal in this partnership?

Apply

5. What would you say to someone who feels intimidated by how non-Christians respond to their Christian faith? Would you listen to your own advice?

6. "Christ in you, the hope of glory." Spell out the privileges of being a Christian. How can we help one another to be reminded of them?

Explore More | OPTIONAL

Read Acts 16:16-34

- How do we see Paul's teaching in Colossians being lived out in his life?

Investigate

Read Colossians 2:1-7

7. How can Paul be "struggling for" the Colossians when he has never met them? (See also Colossians 4:12.)

Paul's message is one that offers "the full riches of complete understanding", and "all the treasures of wisdom" (2:2-3). Just as he did in chapter 1, Paul emphasises the truth that the gospel of Jesus provides everything we need for life with God.

8. Why is it so important for the Colossians to understand that the gospel provides everything (2:4-5)?

9. What is Paul's advice to the Colossians in verses 6-7? Try to summarise it in your own words.

Apply

10. How can we be deceived into thinking that the message of Jesus is not enough for us?

11. Why is it important to be "overflowing with thankfulness"?

Getting Personal | OPTIONAL

It is easy to say that Jesus is the centre of our lives—but how central is he to your daily decision-making, your ambitions and your priorities in life?

Are you in all honesty seeking to follow Paul's commands in verses 6-7?

What could you do differently or start doing as a result?

---

12. From what you have learned so far, discuss how to respond to the following "fine-sounding arguments", so popular today.
    - "It is just intolerant, sinful pride to view your beliefs as true and all others as false and wrong."
    - "Jesus isn't obsessed with religious categories. It doesn't matter to him what faith we choose to label ourselves by. What matters is our love and service to our fellow men."

Pray

Thank God for…

- *the ways in which Jesus has been enough for you this week.*

Ask God to…

- *help you continue to live in Christ and to see through fine-sounding arguments.*

4

Jesus Our Fullness

Colossians 2:8-23

The Story So Far...

Growing in the Christian life is about understanding and relying on what God has done for us in Christ.

We can be confident in Jesus because of who he is—the full image of God—and what he has done—dying to reconcile a rebellious world to God.

Because Jesus is fully God and his victory is total, it is foolish and useless to move on from him. Instead, we should grow stronger in our love for and obedience to him.

Talkabout

1. What images spring to mind with words like "holiness" and "spirituality"?

Paul now draws together some of the big ideas from the last three sections—applying the significance of Jesus' identity more closely to the lives of the Colossians and the struggles they are facing.

Investigate

📖 **Read Colossians 2:8-15**

DICTIONARY

Written code / legal indebtedness (v 14): God's law (which is "against us" because we haven't kept it).

Powers and authorities (v 15): spiritual beings that are opposed to God.

2. In what ways is the message of Christ different from the hollow and deceptive philosophies of human tradition (v 8)?

Paul is not referring to pagan thinking here—in fact he is challenging the mindset that insists on Gentile converts to Christ having to keep the Jewish law (hence the imagery of circumcision).

3. Read Genesis 17:9-14. What was the purpose of circumcision in the Old Testament?

   - So what does Paul mean by the "circumcision done by Christ" (Colossians 2:11)?

4. What three enemies are destroyed by Jesus' death on the cross (v 13-15)? How has this been achieved?

5. How does the cross now make the desire to keep the Jewish law merely an expression of human tradition?

Apply

6. Many today suggest that it is arrogant to be confident that you are right with God. How would you respond to them?

Getting Personal | OPTIONAL

The writer to the Hebrews speaks of having the "full assurance of faith" (Hebrews 10:22). Is this something that you have? If so, praise God for it! If not, what is preventing it?

Investigate

Read Colossians 2:16-23

DICTIONARY

New Moon celebration (v 16): a particular religious festival.
False humility (v 18): appearing humble to make yourself look good!

Sensual indulgence (v 23): ignoring God so that you can do something that makes you feel good.

---

7. Why is the Jewish law no longer needed?

8. What are the spiritual dangers for someone who tries to keep the law in this way (v 17-19)?

9. Why does the rule-keeping referred to by Paul fail to have the desired effect (v 20-23)?

Explore More | OPTIONAL

The relationship that Christians have with the Jewish law is a complex issue, since God was obviously the one to reveal it! Jesus tackled precisely this issue in the Sermon on the Mount.

Read Matthew 5:17-18

- How did Jesus understand his relationship to the law?

Apply

10. Christians today can fall into the same trap as the false teachers in Colossae. What are some of the unnecessary rules or purely cultural conventions that we often expect new Christians to keep?

- Is there anything you as an individual, or as a church, need to change or stop doing as a result?

11. Are you in danger of adding to Christ and his work? Look at the following statements. How do they make you feel, and how would you respond?
    - "If I don't start the day with prayer and reading my Bible, everything else goes wrong."
    - "Christians spend too much time talking to God and not enough time just patiently waiting to hear his still, small voice."
    - "I didn't feel I was truly following Christ until I gave up the trappings of materialism—my car, the TV, eating meat. The simple life brings me closer to God."

Pray

Thank God for…

- *the freedom from human regulations and expectations that we have in Christ.*

Ask God to…

- *help you have the full assurance of faith, having confidence in Christ's finished work on the cross.*

5

Jesus Our Lifestyle

Colossians 3:1 - 4:1

The Story So Far...

Growing in the Christian life is about understanding and relying on what God has done for us in Christ.

We can be confident in Jesus because of who he is—the full image of God—and what he has done—dying to reconcile a rebellious world to God.

Because Jesus is fully God and his victory is total, it is foolish and useless to move on from him. Instead, we should grow stronger in our love for and obedience to him.

Through the cross, Christ has done everything we need to be reconciled to God. If we add anything to him, we'll only subtract our confidence!

Talkabout

1. If you were to ask some non-Christians what they think of churches and Christians they have known, how would they respond? Do you think their opinions are fair?

Investigate

Read Colossians 3:1-4

Paul has given us an astounding account of who Jesus is, and what he has done for us. He now spells out the implications of these truths for how his followers should think and therefore live.

2. What has already happened to believers?

- What will happen in the future to believers?

3. So what should be the thing that drives a Christian's thoughts and actions?

4. How is it possible to say that a Christian has already been raised with Christ? How can we know that this has happened?

Read Colossians 3:5-14

DICTIONARY

Idolatry (v 5): worshipping and serving something other than God, instead of him.
Wrath (v 6): right anger.
Malice (v 8): desire to harm someone.
Scythian (v 11): an ancient people.
Virtues (v 14): good qualities.

5. Find the expressions that talk about giving up the old way of life. What does each of them mean?

6. Find the expressions that describe the way a believer should take up a new way of life. What extra motives for change does Paul mention here?

7. What do these phrases suggest that the change to living a new life will be like? What extra insight does verse 10 give into how this change takes place?

8. What should a church actually look like, according to verses 11-14? Why?

Getting Personal | OPTIONAL

We all have our own areas of frequent temptation and failure. Which of the sins outlined in 3:5-11 are particular issues for you? Which virtues require particular effort? Make a concerted and prayerful effort to work on these in the coming week.

Apply

9. What makes setting "our hearts on things above" difficult? How can we encourage one another to keep a heavenly perspective?

10. How will these verses help you to resolve conflicts and disputes affecting the unity of your church or small group?

Investigate

Read Colossians 3:15 – 4:1

DICTIONARY

Admonish (3:16): challenge firmly.

Reverence (v 22): respect and awe.

Paul now moves to more general recommendations for community life. Notice that these go beyond simply what we do in church together. This is about the whole of our lives, seven days a week.

11. What are the three essential ingredients for healthy life (v 15, 16, 17)?

12. Look through the "household code" in 3:18 – 4:1. How does the Christian attitude to relationships differ from modern views about personal rights?

13. What Paul says here was just as challengingly countercultural in the 1st century as it is now. What is the most important truth for slaves and masters to remember? How does this affect their relationship?

Getting Personal | OPTIONAL

Identify one personal relationship you are struggling with at the moment. What command do you need to obey?

If you are able, share the need with the group so they can pray for and encourage you.

Pray

Thank God...

- *for the joy of knowing that if you know Christ, you have been raised with him and you are a member of God's chosen people, holy and dearly loved.*
- *for the change that God has already begun to bring in your life.*

Ask God...

- *for the ability to set your heart on things above and thus to put off the old self and put on the new self.*
- *for God's peace to rule and God's word to dwell richly in your heart.*
- *to build up the life of the Christian community that you belong to.*

6

Jesus Our Ministry

Colossians 4:2-18

The Story So Far...

We can be confident in Jesus because of who he is—the full image of God—and what he has done—dying to reconcile a rebellious world to God.

Because Jesus is fully God and his victory is total, it is foolish and useless to move on from him. Instead, we should grow stronger in our love for and obedience to him.

Through the cross, Christ has done everything we need to be reconciled to God. If we add anything to him, we'll only subtract our confidence!

A Christian's lifestyle reflects the victory Christ has won for us. Every aspect of our personal, family and community life and relationships will be changed.

Talkabout

1. Who are the people who have influenced you most in your Christian walk? What aspects of their lives and ministry made them such an influence?

Investigate

Read Colossians 4:2-6

Having spent some time teaching about building authentic Christian communities, Paul now turns his attention to our relationship with God and the world beyond the church.

2. How do these verses give us guidance…
   - in our prayer priorities?
   - in our outreach?

3. What is the significance of Paul's use of the expression "the mystery of Christ"? (Compare with 1:27.)

4. Despite the costs involved, why can we be confident when we share the gospel with others?

Apply

5. What practical steps can we take to ensure that…
   - we pray with these priorities?

- we are proclaiming the mystery of Christ clearly?

- we fill our conversation with the salt of grace?

Investigate

📖 **Read Colossians 4:7-18**

DICTIONARY

Vouch for (v 13): guarantee you can trust.

While we might find a passage like this harder to relate to than some others, we should remember that it would have brought real encouragement to the Colossians. Even here, though, there are many things to learn.

6. What virtues do the individuals Paul mentions have in common?

7. What do we learn about the nature of and priorities for prayer from the description of Epaphras in verses 12-13?

8. Why do you think Paul signs off with a reminder of his chains (v 18)?

Explore More | OPTIONAL

Read verse 14 and 2 Timothy 4:10

- What can we learn from the story of Demas?

Getting Personal | OPTIONAL

Is there a person or a group that you are wrestling in prayer for? If not, start now! Determine to pray regularly, passionately and persistently for them.

Apply

9. Paul's description of his friends focuses on their hard work and service for the gospel. How can we encourage one another to persevere in our service of the Lord, his people and those who do not yet know him?

Investigate

10. How does the prayer of Epaphras (4:12) sum up the big message of the letter to the Colossians? Write a sentence summarising the main point Paul has been trying to convey to them.

Apply

11. What advice (from Colossians) would you give the following people?
    - A timid young Christian who wants to be more confident as a believer.

    - Someone who claims to have discovered "something new" in the Christian life.

    - Someone who wants to know how to grow as a Christian.

Pray

Thank God...

- *for the open doors God has provided us with for passing the gospel on to others.*
- *for the individuals who have made an impact on your own Christian walk.*

Ask God...

- *for watchful and thankful prayer lives.*
- *for opportunities to explain the mystery of Christ.*
- *to give you the desire and strength to work hard and sacrificially in the work of Christ.*

7

Jesus Our Unity

Philemon v 1-25

Talkabout

Christ has reconciled us to himself and to each other. But it's one thing to believe that and another to live it out!

1. When is it especially challenging to live with peace and grace towards each other?

Paul's letter to Philemon gives us a striking example of a challenge to someone's discipleship. Is the grace and peace that Paul talked about in Colossians really realistic and workable? Is Philemon willing to be reconciled to a fellow believer even though that feels very hard?

Investigate

📖 **Read Philemon v 1-12**

DICTIONARY

Archippus (v 2): a Christian in Colossae, mentioned in Colossians 4:17.

Onesimus (v 10): this name literally means "useful".

2. According to verses 4-7, how is Philemon already putting his faith into action?

   - Where does Paul see room for growth?

3. We can see this as a real-life example of Colossians 1:10 and 3:10. How so?

In verse 8 Paul gets to the point of his letter: an appeal on behalf of someone called Onesimus.

4. Write down what we have learned about Paul, Philemon and Onesimus by the end of verse 12.
   - Paul

   - Philemon

   - Onesimus

We later discover that Onesimus is a slave belonging to Philemon. (See verse 16.) Onesimus has run away and taken refuge with Paul—who is in prison, probably in Ephesus. While with Paul, Onesimus has become a Christian.

5. Before we move on to what Paul wants Philemon to do, look again at verses 1-12 and consider how Paul talks about these two friends. What are they to him? And why (as far as we can tell)?

Apply

6. Reflect on the relationships in your own church. How similar or different are they to Paul's relationships? Use the following questions to help you.
   - In what ways are people being partners in the faith (v 6)?
   - How is that partnership deepening people's understanding or knowledge?
   - How are people refreshing each other's hearts (v 7)?

- Do you speak to each other on the basis of love (v 9)—Christ's love, which reconciles us to God and to each other? Are there any relationships that have more to do with authority or power than love?

- Are people treating each other as spiritual family members (v 10)? What does that look like in the modern Western world?

Getting Personal | OPTIONAL

Think about the people you know at church. Whose heart can you refresh this week and how?

Investigate

Read Philemon v 12-25

For a slave, running away was punishable by death. In his culture, Philemon would seem to have every right to be very angry with Onesimus.

7. So why is Paul sending Onesimus back to Philemon? What is he hoping Philemon will do?

8. What reasons does Paul give Philemon for this? Think about...
   - the changes in Onesimus (v 11-12, 16).

- God's plan (v 15-16).

- financial considerations (v 18).

- Philemon's relationship with Paul (v 17, 19-20).

Explore More | OPTIONAL

Centuries later, Paul's words in verse 16 became an anti-slavery slogan. The question "Am I not a man and a brother?", coupled with an image of an African man kneeling in chains, was a crucial campaign tool in the 18th-century abolition movement in Britain.

Paul did not speak out against slavery as an institution. In Colossians 3:22-24 he encourages enslaved people to serve Christ within their servile status. Yet here in Philemon, we can see that Paul did have a radical view on slavery. He treated Onesimus and Philemon as equals—describing them in very similar terms. In Christ, there is no slave or free (Colossians 3:11)—there are only brothers and sisters.

- Imagine yourself in the shoes of a slave owner in the 1st century. How would you have responded to Paul's words in Colossians 3:11 and Philemon v 15-16?
- What about if you were a slave—how would you have responded then?
- Now imagine you are Paul, explaining to a slave owner and a slave why they are actually equals in Christ. What would you say? Base your answer on the Bible.

9. How does all of this illustrate what Paul taught in Colossians 3:11-15? Draw out specific links.

10. Paul closes with a message of grace (Philemon v 25). How have we seen him exemplify and encourage the grace (undeserved love) of Jesus in this letter?

Slavery was so normal and integral to life in the Roman world that very few recognised its inhumanity. It was one of their biggest blind spots, which is why it would take so long for Paul's radical approach to cut through.

11. What might be our blind spots today—aspects of modern life that we assume are normal and acceptable, despite challenges from the gospel? In particular, in what ways does Jesus' radical message of reconciliation impact us?

- In those areas of life, how can we cultivate the kind of love, grace and peace that Paul shows in his letter to Philemon?

Getting Personal | OPTIONAL

This portrait of grace demands that we examine our own lives and communities for signs of "ungrace". Are there fellow believers with whom you refuse to be reconciled? Or be associated? Or share your life? Are you willing to think again?

12. What is the one thing you most want to remember from your study of Colossians and Philemon?

Pray

Pray for the relationships within your families, your church and the wider community. Ask Jesus to reveal the glory of his grace by the way you treat one another. Confess where you have fallen short and ask for the Spirit's help to transform you more into the likeness of Christ.

Colossians & Philemon

Confident Christianity

LEADER'S GUIDE

Leader's Guide: Introduction

This Leader's Guide includes guidance for every question. It will provide background information and help you if you get stuck. For each session, you'll also find the following:

The Big Idea: The main point of the session, in brief. This is what you should be aiming to have fixed in people's minds by the end of the session!

Summary: An overview of the passage you're reading together.

Optional Extra: Usually this is an introductory activity that ties in with the main theme of the Bible study and is designed to break the ice at the beginning of a session. Or it may be a "homework project" that people can tackle during the week.

Occasionally the Leader's Guide includes an extra follow-up question, printed in ***italics***. This doesn't appear in the main study guide but could be a useful add-on to help your group get to the answer or go deeper.

Here are a few key principles to bear in mind as you prepare to lead:

- Don't just read out the answers from the Leader's Guide. Ideally, you want the group to discover these answers from the Bible for themselves.
- Keep drawing people back to the passage you're studying. People may come up with answers based on their experiences or on teaching they've heard in the past, but the point of this study is to listen to God's word itself—so keep directing your group to look at the text.
- Make sure everyone finishes the session knowing how the passage is relevant for them. We do Bible study so that our lives can be changed by what we hear from God's word. So, **Apply** questions aren't just an add-on—they're a vital part of the session.

Finally, remember that your group is unique! You should feel free to use this Good Book Guide in a way that works for them. If they're a quiet bunch, you might want to spend longer on the **Talkabout** question. If they love to get creative, try using mind-mapping or doodling to kick-start some of your discussions. If your time is limited, you can choose to skip **Explore More** or split the whole session into two. Adapt the material in whatever way you think will help your group get the most out of God's word.

1

Jesus Our Confidence

Colossians 1:1-14

The Big Idea

Growing in the Christian life is about understanding and relying on what God has done for us in Christ.

Summary

Colossae was in what is now south-west Turkey, not far from Laodicea and near the great Ephesus road. Paul writes this letter from his prison in Rome to a church that he has never visited but about which he has heard fantastic reports from their leader and founder, Epaphras. (Compare 1:7; 4:12.) He writes the letter both to encourage the church and to alert them to the dangers of false teachers (some of whom have sought to infiltrate the church). They had started well in their Christian walk—they clearly understood the relationship between Christian faith, love and hope (1:4-5), and this provided them with a firm foundation for their lives in Christ. The important thing is that they continue to understand and trust in Christ's victory at the cross (v 12-14), which will then impact their daily living (v 9-11). This is why Paul is so keen to pray for them and to write this letter.

Guidance for Questions

1. **What things do you give thanks to God for and/or pray for the most?**
   If you keep a prayer diary as a group, it may be worth reading out some of the things you have regularly prayed for. The point of this exercise is to show that the things we often pray for—illness, guidance questions, etc.—are very different from the things Paul prays for.

2. **What evidence is there for the Colossians' conversion?**
   Epaphras has reported the significant difference that the Colossians' conversions have made to their lives. They responded to the gospel with trust in Christ and a love for fellow believers.
   NOTE: "Saints" in the Bible are all those in Christ and not those who have reached a higher grade of discipleship.

3. **Read verse 5. In what ways does hope motivate faith and love, do you think?**
   Christian hope marks the gospel out as unique—for it brings total confidence in an eternal future, simply because of what Christ has achieved on our behalf. We contribute nothing. If we did, there could be no confidence. As we consider this future, we are thrown back on Christ's mercy and recognise we have no option but to trust him. This then gives us the freedom to love

others without the burden of trying to earn God's approval.

4. **The New Testament describes conversion to Christ in various ways. What is unusual about Paul's description in verses 5-8?**
   Paul talks about the gospel (like a living thing—a seed growing and bearing fruit) as the most important thing.

- **Why is this change not simply a matter of intellectual understanding?**
  Conversion here is described as hearing "the word of truth" (v 5), understanding "God's grace in all its truth" (v 6) and learning "it from Epaphras" (v 7). There is therefore an intellectual element to conversion. But it can never stop there—for it leads to "love in the Spirit" (v 8), which is evidence of a changed life.

5. **What does Paul specifically pray for in verse 9?**
   That God would fill them with "the knowledge of his will", and give them "all spiritual wisdom and understanding". Knowing God's will comes through the wisdom and knowledge of God that we derive from the gospel.

6. **Why are these things important? (See verses 10-11.)**
   Because the false teachers in Colossae were undermining the completed work of Christ (as we will soon see), it was essential for Paul to root these believers in the gospel. Firm convictions were needed if they were to bear fruit and grow (v 10), and especially to endure (v 11). Note that this is not philosophical knowledge—it is about a relationship with God.

7. **What is the link between knowledge and wisdom, and good works (v 9-10)?**
   Throughout the Bible, there is a clear link between doctrine and ethics—between what we think and how we behave. Wrong thinking invariably leads to wrong living. This is all the more true when it comes to our understanding of the character of God.

8. **Note the tense of these verses (past, present or future). List all the things that the Father has done. How did he achieve them?**
   The past tenses are the key to a Christian's assurance. They point us to the reality that God has already done everything we need to be saved: He has "qualified" us for heaven (v 12), "rescued" us from darkness (v 13), and "brought" us into the kingdom of the Son (v 13). These were all ultimately achieved at the cross—where Jesus, once and for all time, completed his divine rescue mission.

9. **So how can a Christian have confidence when faced with the challenge to endure with patience and joy? (See verse 11.)**
   We all have days when the going gets tough. But because God is the one who has achieved the victory (v 13), a Christian's ability to endure, whatever

gruelling challenges lie ahead, is all about depending on what God has done for us in Christ.

Explore More

- ***Read 1 Thessalonians 1:1-10. What are the similarities and differences between Paul's prayers in this passage and the one in Colossians 1:3-14?***
  In 1 Thessalonians, Paul also focuses his thanksgiving to God on the outworking of these Christians' faith, love and hope (1 Thessalonians 1:3). Just as with the Colossians, each of these three virtues has a practical impact, producing "work", "labour" and "endurance". Furthermore, there is a parallel in the difference that their hope makes—for that is what enables them to serve the living and true God (as opposed to dumb idols) as they wait for Jesus' return (1 Thessalonians 1:9-10).

  But there are subtle differences between the two passages. In Colossians, Paul is already flagging up some of his concerns about their gospel convictions. Colossians 1:11-14 suggest that the Colossians were looking elsewhere for strength to endure. In 1 Thessalonians, Paul is thrilled about the impact their conversions have had on the wider church (e.g. 1 Thessalonians 1:8). Both churches have started well, and this has given Paul real encouragement and grounds for praise.

- ***OPTIONAL: What grounds for encouragement and praise do you find in your church?***

10. **What are the challenges from this passage for our priorities in prayer?**
    Compare your answers to question 1! Will we share Paul's commitment to praying for Christians' wisdom and gospel understanding?

11. **What will the cost be for us, if we are to be faithful followers of Christ?**
    Discipleship costs: we need endurance not only in tough circumstances (which Paul clearly assumes will come), but also our challenge is, daily, to find strength and joy in God rather than always trying to avoid suffering and difficulty.

12. **How can we contribute to the gospel bearing fruit? (Clue: How did it bear fruit in the Colossians' lives, according to verse 6?)**
    The gospel bore fruit in the Colossians' lives when they heard and understood the grace of God, and showed love in the Spirit. We can support gospel growth by…
    - teaching the gospel ourselves.
    - supporting preachers like Epaphras.
    - praying for gospel growth and fruit in the lives of others.
    - demonstrating the fruit of the gospel in our lives (i.e. love, holiness, joy etc.).

2

Jesus Our Lord

Colossians 1:15-23

The Big Idea

We can be confident in Jesus because of who he is: the full and final Word, who reveals God's character, authority and purposes in his world; and who shows what he has done—he has reconciled a rebellious world to God through his death on the cross.

Summary

The false teachers in Colossae clearly undermined core gospel truths. It is not that they never talked about Jesus. The problem was that they subtly shifted people's focus from the biblical and historical Jesus. They undermined his full identity and finished work on the cross by implying that coming to Christ in conversion was not enough to have confidence for the future and eternity. So in these momentous paragraphs, Paul lifts our eyes to the wonders of who Jesus is and what he has done. Having done that, Paul unpacks the astounding confidence that is every Christian's right and privilege. This provides the foundation for the next section: stick to Jesus for the whole of your Christian walk; don't think you can graduate from him. (See Colossians 2:6-7.)

NOTE: Some people may raise the question of whether all people are saved because of the wording in 1:20—"Reconcile all things". It is true that one day the whole of creation will be united in recognising the lordship of Jesus (see Philippians 2:11). But, as the following verses in Colossians make plain, there are still two ways to go. Those who love him will bow the knee gladly; those who have rejected him must still be judged.

Optional Extra

Think about a film or TV portrayal of Christ that you have all seen, perhaps showing a clip from one of them. How does it help or hinder our understanding of Jesus' identity and mission? What value (if any) is there in such attempts to portray Christ?

Guidance for Questions

1. **If they give Jesus any thought at all, how do your friends and colleagues tend to view him? What relevance would they say that he has for life today?**
   Answers will vary—some will be positive, but probably most will be negative.

- ***OPTIONAL: If we live among people who treat Jesus as irrelevant, what effect can this have on our view of him?***

2. **Underline or write down each time Paul uses the words "all", "every"**

and "full". What point is Paul making?

He is stressing the sufficiency of Jesus for everything—he is fully God; he made everything and is the Redeemer of everything; he thus has authority over everything; he sustains everything; he is the first to rise from the dead; he brings real and lasting peace with God.

3. **Spot the parallels between the two halves of this passage.**
   See table below.

- **Why is it important that Jesus is God's image?**
  Being "God's image" effectively means that he makes the invisible God visible. He provides the greatest window into the character and purposes of God that the world has ever known. See John 14:9.

  NOTE: Being "firstborn over all creation" in no sense implies that he is a part of creation, as if he was the same as all other creatures. Not only would that contradict everything Paul says in this paragraph, but it also misunderstands the term. To be firstborn in the ancient world meant being the primary inheritor in the family. Jesus thus has a Son's rights (compare Colossians 1:12-13) over all creation because of who he is, but also because he is its Creator.

4. **Reread verses 13-17. Paul makes astonishing claims about what God has done through Jesus (v 13-14). What qualifies Jesus to bring about this rescue (v 15)?**
   Most people have no difficulty with the concept of God creating and sustaining the universe. What is truly mind-blowing is the Bible's claim that this same creating, all-sustaining God became a human being: none other than Jesus of Nazareth. What qualifies Jesus is that he is God.

	Verses 15-17 (Creation)	Verses 18-20 (Rescue)
How is Jesus described?	• Image of the invisible God • Firstborn over all creation • He is before all things	• Head of the body, the church • Firstborn from among the dead • God pleased to have all his fullness dwell in him
What does Jesus achieve?	• All things created by him (and that really does mean everything!) • All things created for him • All things hold together in him	• Firstborn from among the dead (so has supremacy) • God pleased to reconcile all things to himself through Christ • Made peace through his blood, shed on the cross

5. **How does the universe depend on Jesus? Describe the past and present aspects of this relationship.**
   - Past: Jesus was the one at the beginning: he was before all things; he created all things.
   - Present: He holds everything together, and it is for him that everything exists.

6. **Why does Paul spell out that Christ's authority even extends to human rulers (v 16)? Clue: Look at 4:18!)**

   Paul was writing from prison. The Roman world was hostile to the gospel and its messengers. In the face of such persecution, it was vital to cling to a confidence in the sovereignty of Christ. His lordship extends even to those who sent Paul to prison in the first place. We can draw real comfort in the midst of suffering.

7. **Reread 1:18-20. Why is it important we understand that Jesus is the "head of the body, the church"?**

   If we don't acknowledge that Jesus is the head of the church, then we will inevitably go wrong. We will make reason or tradition or our leaders into the head, and so compromise the purpose and character of the church. It seems from chapter 2 that this is the danger the Colossians were wrestling with. If Jesus is Lord of the church, then his word will be our rule and guide.

8. **What is the extent of Jesus' victory on the cross (v 20)?**

   The surprise is that Jesus' victory is cosmic: "all things" (whether on earth or in heaven) are reconciled.

- **How would you explain how his death on the cross makes peace?**

  Human rebellion against God caused a profound dislocation and rupture throughout God's creation. Jesus' death repairs and restores it all. Peace comes because of the shedding of his blood—his death in our place, taking the punishment for rebellion we deserve onto himself so that we might be restored to friendship with God. Hebrews 9:19-26 expresses these truths clearly.

Explore More

- ***Read John 1:1-14 and Hebrews 1:1-4. What do these add to our understanding of Jesus' identity and mission?***

  With Colossians 1, these passages are the classic New Testament witnesses to Jesus' incarnation—he is clearly seen to be both fully divine and fully human. John 1 echoes Genesis 1, with a similar cosmic scope to Colossians 1:
  - *The Creator God of Genesis is none other than the Word himself—who is God.*
  - *God became human when he made his dwelling among us. John 1:14 literally means he "tabernacled" with us, picking up on*

Old Testament imagery of the place where people went to meet with God—the tabernacle/temple. Hebrews 1 has a focus on how Jesus completes the process of revelation, which started in the Old Testament.

---

9. How might you respond to a Christian friend who says, "All you need to know about Jesus is that he died to forgive us"?
The key is the cosmic scope of God's purposes—the cross is not simply about forgiving someone or "getting them to heaven". It is designed, in one great decisive victory, to restore everything in the universe to the lordship of Christ.

10. What would you say to a friend who thinks Jesus is irrelevant?
Jesus is not just a "special friend" for Christians. The resurrection here points to Jesus' supremacy. He is the Lord of all, whether people recognise that or not, whether you think he is relevant or not. What Jesus achieved is the only way that all the problems and agonies of the fallen world will be overcome.

11. What has changed in the Colossians' lives, and how did that come about?
The alienation from God experienced by the whole of creation had been the experience of the individual Colossians as well. But through hearing the gospel of the victorious death of Christ, they were reconciled to God and presented "holy in his sight". This is what they are to continue trusting in.

12. What will a confident Christian look like? (See verse 23.)
A confident Christian…

- "keeps" their faith. That is, they continue to believe the truths of the gospel and also live by it. The truth that Jesus Christ is the Lord of all and the very purpose for the existence of the world will be the truth that dominates their decisions and choices.
- "is steadfast". That is, they are prepared to fight or contend for this truth, even when it costs them. They will hold to it even if they are persecuted for it. They won't just follow the latest fad in spirituality or go looking for other things outside Jesus, because everything is in him.
- "is not moved from the hope of the gospel". They are confident that in Christ they are fully accepted by God and sure they will live with him for ever. This gives them the ability to endure suffering and hardship now, and to be happy not to seek after what the world has to offer, because they know that they will have it all and more besides, in eternity with Christ.

13. What difficulties do you face in proclaiming the gospel to others?
Many people are either ignorant of or couldn't care less about the claims of Christ. What's more, many have precious little hope for the future.

This passage reminds us of God's cosmic purposes—and the fact that in Christ he has already won. People's rejection of him doesn't change that fact. We are simply servants of the message of Jesus' lordship (as Paul was in 1:23). To put it bluntly, Christ's lordship does not depend on my ability or failures in passing on the message.

- **How does this passage encourage and strengthen you for that?** Encourage people to relate specific verses to their specific day-to-day lives.

3

Jesus Our Rock

Colossians 1:24 -2:7

The Big Idea

Because Jesus is fully God and his victory is total, it is fruitless and foolish to move on from him—instead we should grow deeper roots in him.

Summary

Paul was prepared to suffer in order to proclaim Christ because it meant building up his body (the church). For Paul, the real privilege was to explain the wonders of God's purposes to the non-Jewish (Gentile) world: namely, that a Jewish Messiah (or King) was in fact the ruler of the universe. Jesus is the focal point for all Christian ministry. Even though such ministry brings hardships, Paul is confident that God is at work in him, providing all the energy he needs to carry out his ministry.

The threat to the Colossians' faith is what particularly provokes Paul to write this letter. There are those who undermine Jesus' finished work by saying that a believer needs to supplement what Christ has done, perhaps through wisdom that is to be found elsewhere (compare 2:3 and 4). But such people deceive by their "fine-sounding arguments". Paul would love to teach the Colossians in person—but for the time being he can only write. The heart of his message is therefore in 2:6-7—don't move on from Christ; go deeper into Christ.

Optional Extra

Find a hymn or song that faces up to the realities of suffering and disappointment in the Christian life. Play it to, or sing it with, the group and discuss the extent to which it puts suffering in a right, biblical perspective. (E.g. Hymns: *Abide with me;*

Father, hear the prayer we offer. Modern songs are harder to find on these themes, but try: Matt Redman's *Blessed be your name* or Stuart Townend's *We have sung our songs of victory.*)

Guidance for Questions

1. **What things shake your confidence as a Christian?**
   Try to draw out a whole range of issues:
   - Intellectual attacks, e.g. documentaries or books that cast doubt on the Bible or the historicity of Jesus.
   - Disappointments, e.g. the failures of Christian leaders that you look up to.
   - Seemingly inexplicable suffering.

   NOTE: Listen carefully to what people say, as it may reveal real issues they are struggling with. People can often talk in an abstract way about something that they are really wrestling with deep inside. Make a note to follow up with a personal conversation anything that has raised concern.

2. **What enabled Paul to persevere and even rejoice in the midst of his sufferings?**
   In no sense did Paul enjoy suffering, nor did he rejoice at the fact of other people suffering. That would be absurd. Suffering is simply part of Christian discipleship, but the joy is to be found in the perspective and the purpose that Christ gives suffering. Paul suffered for his efforts to make the gospel known to the Gentile world. Knowing that they now know "this mystery" (v 27) is what makes it all worthwhile and joyful.

3. **What exactly is the "mystery" God has chosen to reveal to the Gentiles, and why is it so remarkable?**
   The "mystery" is about Christ being made known to the whole world, including the Gentiles. Remarkably, the God who made the universe and sustains it chooses to make his home in us and to take us to glory.

4. **Spell out the part God plays in the preaching of the gospel, and the part Paul plays. What is the ultimate goal in this partnership?**
   - *God's part:* The church is Christ's body—his agent on earth. He is the one suffering through its sufferings (compare Paul's conversion experience in Acts 9:4), but he is therefore also the one to commission the preaching of the gospel. It is his mystery that was hidden, and it is now disclosed by him (v 27). He is the one working powerfully within his agents as they proclaim Christ (v 29).
   - *Paul's part:* In the light of that, Paul and all who follow him in Christian ministry are merely servants who seek to present the word faithfully and in its fullness (v 25) and must be prepared to suffer for it (v 24).
   - The goal is for people to be presented perfect in Christ (1:28)—it is disciples that God seeks, not merely converts.

5. **What would you say to someone who feels intimidated by how non-Christians respond to their Christian faith? Would you listen to your own advice?**
   This is a totally understandable fear—it would be strange if we didn't feel it. However, we are called to follow Jesus—we can't expect to avoid something of what he endured (compare John 15:20). That never means he has abandoned us or that what we go through is indefinite or futile. Colossians constantly reminds us of God's sovereign plan and sustaining power for those who trust in him.

6. **"Christ in you, the hope of glory." Spell out the privileges of being a Christian. How can we help one another to be reminded of them?**
   In the present, we have the astonishing confidence of "Christ in you". That idea dovetails with the idea of a Christian being "in Christ" (1:28). There is a strong sense of security in knowing both truths. Then we have the future perspective given by "the hope of glory"—this is no pipe dream but confidence because it all depends on God. Still, this can all seem unreal when things get tough. That is why we need to read our Bibles, be part of Christian meetings and be involved in Christian service—so that we are constantly drawn back to spiritual realities.

Explore More

- ***How do we see Paul's teaching in Colossians being lived out in his life?***
  Paul and Silas are preaching the gospel in Philippi. Acceptance gives way to opposition and hostility as the gospel does its work. The first three converts are a wealthy businesswoman, a possessed slave girl and a jailer and his family—showing how the gospel of God reaches out to everyone. Paul and Silas bear their suffering with joy—singing hymns in the stocks—and God wonderfully blesses their faithful witness.

7. **How can Paul be "struggling for" the Colossians when he has never met them? (See also Colossians 4:12.)**
   Long distances are no bar to Paul's ministry to the Colossian Christians, nor is the fact he has never met them. Presumably (from the reference to Epaphras in 4:12), Paul is struggling for them in devoted prayer for them, as well as by writing this letter. But see 2:4! Paul is struggling for them by contending for the gospel message. This encourages Christians everywhere (1:23).

8. **Why is it so important for the Colossians to understand that the gospel provides everything (2:4-5)?**
   If we don't understand the fullness of what we have in Christ, we will be easy prey for the deceptions of false

teachers because they are offering to supplement Christ with their own ways of thinking or living, which will offer an easier life or give room for our own pride. The rule is that if you try to add to Jesus, you will always end up taking away from his achievements because, if you have to add anything, it suggests that what he did was inadequate in the first place.

9. **What is Paul's advice to the Colossians in verses 6-7? Try to summarise it in your own words.**
Stick with Jesus (or people's own words to that effect!). There is always more to learn and love about Christ. Continue to grow by being grounded where you started—hence the imagery of a tree putting down strong roots. Thankfulness is a key discipline here because, when we start to look for things to be thankful for, we will always find more than enough in Jesus!

10. **How can we be deceived into thinking that the message of Jesus is not enough for us?**
Deception usually starts with someone making us dissatisfied with the realities of the Christian life, e.g. our struggle with sin. They then offer us a "better way" that will help us over the problem. That's why thankfulness is so important. If we are thankful to God for all he has given us, including the opportunity to suffer for him, then we will not be dissatisfied and hence not prone to deception by false teachers.

There are many examples of this kind of false teaching around. Some say it doesn't matter which religion you turn to for hope —this denies the uniqueness of Christ and implies that we can be reconciled to God without the cross. But some within Christian circles insist that a spiritual experience they have enjoyed should be the norm for all Christians. This can leave people feeling insecure and that somehow their walk with Jesus is lacking. But if we are in Christ, we have it all already, regardless of how we feel or what we experience.

11. **Why is it important to be "overflowing with thankfulness"?**
Gratitude is not just a good thing; it is a key Christian discipline. When we start to look for things to be thankful to God for, we will always find more than enough in Jesus! So it is something that we should do, even if we are not "feeling thankful". It strengthens us against those who would deceive us into thinking we need more than Jesus.

12. **From what you have learned so far, discuss how to respond to the following "fine-sounding arguments", so popular today.**
Each of these arguments attacks the uniqueness of the gospel in reconciling sinners to God. Each one is a deceptive means of giving other faiths and creeds equality with the gospel. The arguments can appear "fine-sounding" because they use half-truths.

- **"It is just intolerant, sinful pride to view your beliefs as true and all others as false and wrong."**
  We can be intolerant and sinfully proud about our beliefs, BUT the key issue is truth. How can we know the gospel is true?
- **"Jesus isn't obsessed with religious categories. It doesn't matter to him what faith we choose to label ourselves by. What matters is our love and service to our fellow men."**
  It's true that Jesus isn't obsessed with religious categories (because all religion fails to reconcile us to God). BUT he calls people of all beliefs to put faith in him alone.

It is important to underline to your group that false teaching will always be plausible in this way, because it will contain things that are true. We need to sort out the truth from the error.

4

Jesus Our Fullness

Colossians 2:8-23

The Big Idea

Christ has done everything we need to be reconciled to God through his death on the cross. If we add anything to Christ, we will only subtract our confidence!

Summary

Paul now goes into much greater detail about the nature of the false teaching prevalent in Colossae. Because of his need to explain the issue of circumcision (2:11), it seems clear that a central element of this was the expectation that Gentile converts keep the Jewish law in its entirety. The arguments for doing this would have seemed sensible and convincing (compare v 4), not least because, of course, the Old Testament law was God's idea in the first place. But Paul uses shocking language to describe the false teachers' approach: for despite the law's divine origins, their insistence on applying it directly to new Gentile believers renders their philosophy one of "human tradition and the basic principles of this world" (v 8).

The key reason for Paul's robust language is that to insist on people adopting human traditions as well as the gospel completely undermines Jesus' victorious achievements at the cross, which, in turn, undermines a Christian's sense of assurance. The cross is no longer "enough" for us to be reconciled to God if a believer has to do certain things in addition. What is more, this tends to feed personal pride and loosens a person's wholehearted dependence on Christ. Finally, and most depressingly, this approach completely fails to deliver what it promises: namely, a lifestyle that is more Christ-like, holy or devoted.

It is vital that the Colossian believers resist this way of thinking. They should not feel pressured or insecure because they do not keep certain festivals or rituals (v 16-17). What matters is what they have in Christ

Optional Extra

Think of any soap-opera or movie characters who are supposed to be Christians. What impression do they give? How accurate is it? How much would you say this is a result of the writers' prejudice, and how much is actually deserved?

Guidance for Questions

1. **What images spring to mind with words like "holiness" and "spirituality"?**
   Common ideas include people who are disconnected from the world, abstinence, emptying your mind, visions, ecstatic singing, killjoys, etc.

2. **In what ways is the message of Christ different from the hollow and deceptive philosophies of human tradition (v 8)?**
   The key thing to identify is the origin of the way of life offered. Christ is from God; the alternatives are all of human invention. Whatever the roots of a particular way of life, if it undermines the work of Christ, then it is by definition not from God. For in Christ, we have God in all his fullness, and if we are Christian, we have Christ in all his fullness. The other major difference would be that the alternatives will sound great, whereas the true gospel will not pull any punches about how difficult it will be.

3. **Read Genesis 17:9-14. What was the purpose of circumcision in the Old Testament?**
   Circumcision was a physical sign of the covenant between God and his people. It showed that a man belonged to God's chosen people. It marked them out as different.

- **So what does Paul mean by the "circumcision done by Christ" (Colossians 2:11)?**
  Instead of a physical act to demonstrate belonging to the community of God, Jesus now does this spiritually—at our conversion when we first trust him ("through your faith in the power of God", v 12). You could see this as simply an alternative description of someone who has Christ in them (1:27) and is in Christ (2:28).

4. **What three enemies are destroyed by Jesus' death on the cross (v 13-15)? How has this been achieved?**
   Through his death, Christ brought forgiveness and reconciliation to God by removing the three major obstacles that lie in a sinner's way:

- Death, which is the inevitable consequence of rebellion against God (v 13).
- Our failure to obey God's standards of perfection as expressed in the law (the "written code ... that stood opposed to us"—v 14).
- The powers and authorities that stand opposed to God and his people (v 15).

He did this by...

- rising from the dead and enabling those in Christ to follow suit (v 13).
- taking the punishment deserved by spiritual failures on himself at the cross (v 14)—sin is never punished twice, which is why we no longer have anything to fear.

Far from being a defeat, ironically, the cross was where God overcame hostile spiritual forces. Paul uses the imagery of a Roman triumph—a great procession of captured enemies through the streets of Rome (v 15).

5. **How does the cross now make the desire to keep the Jewish law merely an expression of human tradition?**

We are naturally drawn to any religion that expects us to contribute good works to earn a place with God, since it appeals to our innate pride to think that our contribution will have an impact. But according to Paul, that is deceptive, hollow, and worldly. Our sin is so serious that it leaves us spiritually dead (v 13)—we cannot possibly contribute anything. We are in dire need of a rescuer, which thankfully we find in Jesus Christ (v 14-15). Going back to these religious ways of feeling safe or helping us feel good about ourselves is not only not helpful but positively harmful.

6. **Many today suggest that it is arrogant to be confident that you are right with God. How would you respond to them?**

The irony is that it is only those who rely on their own performance who are arrogant. To accept that we are in desperate need of forgiveness and that Christ is the only one to pull us out of our predicament requires great humility. However, confidence is a different matter altogether. For the truth is that confidence is only possible if we trust God to do everything we need to be reconciled. If it depended on us for even the smallest part, that confidence would instantly evaporate. Christian assurance is based on what Christ has already done on our behalf, not on what we can do for him.

7. **Why is the Jewish law no longer needed?**

The law was a "shadow" of the things that were to come in Jesus. Now he is here, we have the "reality" (v 17). There is no need to return to the law (v 16). E.g. the sacrificial system no longer applies because Jesus is the final sacrifice; the food laws no longer apply because we now show that we are different to the rest of the world by living a life of love for God and others.

8. **What are the spiritual dangers for someone who tries to keep the law in this way (v 17-19)?**
Their humility will be a sham because they are still arrogantly relying on their own performance to some degree. The "worship of angels" seems to correspond to a strand of false teaching that made much of spiritual experiences. The danger with these is that they only lead further down the path to spiritual pride (v 18), as well as making others feel left out. Worst of all, a focus on personal achievement and experiences erodes dependence on Christ—which eventually leads to losing connection with him altogether (v 19).

- ***OPTIONAL: Share examples of this that you may have seen happen with other Christians or churches, or even in your own church.***

9. **Why does the rule-keeping referred to by Paul fail to have the desired effect (v 20-23)?**
Such rules might help false teachers determine who is in their clique and who is out. But these distinctions have no value from an eternal perspective because they are "based on human commands" (v 20-22). They make someone appear to be holy, but they do nothing to deal with the sinful nature that is at work beneath the surface. The crucial point here is that sin can show itself in very religious ways, just as it can in pagan or irreligious ways.

Explore More

- ***Read Matthew 5:17-18. How did Jesus understand his relationship to the law?***
Jesus was frequently accused of undermining or abolishing the Old Testament law. He clearly refutes that by saying that he has come to fulfil the law, not least because it was God-given. However, his fulfilment of the law has many aspects:
  - *He fulfils the purpose for which it was given—for example, the sacrificial system was designed to be a shadow of what Jesus would achieve on the cross. So even though it is no longer in use, we need to study it in order to understand the cross.*
  - *Uniquely, he kept the law perfectly—he alone succeeded where the Old Testament people of God failed.*
  - *He took on himself the requirements of the law by suffering the punishment demanded by our human failure to be holy.*

---

10. **Christians today can fall into the same trap as the false teachers in Colossae. What are some of the unnecessary rules or purely cultural conventions that we often expect new Christians to keep?**
Our tendency is to twist the good gifts of God and wise habits of the Christian life into things that cause us spiritual problems. So, for

instance, we can easily twist the habit of having a regular devotional time with God into something that determines our status before God. We can think that if we have a quiet time, our day will automatically go better than if we don't, or that God will be more impressed with us. But our standing before God depends entirely on Christ's performance, not ours! We do this with going to church, telling people about Jesus, seeking to be godly, acts of service and mercy and so on.

- **Is there anything you as an individual, or as a church, need to change or stop doing as a result?**
  NOTE: Beware of any tendency in your group to point the finger at others without spending time thinking about how you yourselves, individually and as a church, may be making the same errors. The opposite danger here is that people grumble about things they feel are wrong with their own church. There may be legitimate concerns, but always make sure that any issues are properly dealt with by discussing them with your church leadership, rather than just grumbling about them and leaving them. That can only be counterproductive.

11. **Are you in danger of adding to Christ and his work? Look at the following statements. How do they make you feel, and how would you respond?**
    The three statements reflect the three different ways of adding to Christ's work highlighted in these verses:

- **"If I don't start the day with prayer and reading my Bible, everything else goes wrong."**
  Legalism (v 16-17): Law-keeping makes me feel more acceptable to God.

- **"Christians spend too much time talking to God and not enough time just patiently waiting to hear his still, small voice."**
  Mysticism (v 18-19): Spiritual experiences make me feel more acceptable to God.

- **"I didn't feel I was truly following Christ until I gave up the trappings of materialism—my car, the TV, eating meat. The simple life brings me closer to God."**
  Asceticism (v 20-23): Self-denial makes me feel more acceptable to God.

  People who talk like this can make us feel guilty or unconfident. Help the group see that these are steps backward, not forward!

5

Jesus Our Lifestyle

Colossians 3:1 - 4:1

The Big Idea

A Christian's lifestyle will reflect the victory that Christ has already won on our behalf. There is no aspect of our personal, family and community life and relationships that will not be changed.

Summary

Being rescued by Jesus and having complete assurance as the result of his finished reconciling work is no excuse for an unchanged life. He is now our Lord. He did it all in order to restore everything in the universe to its rightful place under his authority. (Compare 1:18.) We have been raised with Christ and therefore need to live lives that reflect that (3:1-4; then v 5). This impacts our ambitions and desires, our words and deeds. It especially affects our relationships with fellow believers, among whom there should be no discrimination (v 11) or division (v 12-14). For this to happen, we need to depend on Christ all the more and work hard at serving him and his people through everything (v 15-18).

But this lifestyle revolution will not only affect our Christian communities, but also our homes—hence Paul's encouragements to the members of the typical household of his day: wives and husbands, parents and children, slaves and masters. These are all to be characterised by selfless service and other-person-centredness, just as Jesus was.

Optional Extra

Give pairs these scenarios, for them to stage a one-minute drama for the rest of the group. This introduces the idea of conflict and the way we argue for our "rights".

- A boss and an employee: one arguing for a pay rise, the other bringing up poor effort and time-keeping at work.
- A child and a parent: a "discussion" about staying out later than usual.
- A husband and a wife: talking about the household budget overspend.

You may like to discuss these scenarios at the end to see what difference it would make if Paul's teaching were followed.

Guidance for Questions

1. **If you were to ask some non-Christians what they think of churches and Christians they have known, how would they respond? Do you think their opinions are fair?**
   Answers may include: hypocrites; people who need a psychological crutch; so heavenly-minded they are no earthly use (but see v 2!); outdated; weird.

- ***OPTIONAL: Why do people have such a bad impression of church?***

2. **What has already happened to believers?**
We died with Christ (v 3), and we were raised with Christ (v 1). Our real life is safe with Christ in heaven (v 3). All this is in the past tense. It is done and finished!

- **What will happen in the future to believers?**
In the future, when Jesus appears—a reference to his second coming—we will be taken to be with him.

3. **So what should be the thing that drives a Christian's thoughts and actions?**
In Colossians 2, Paul outlines the finished work of Jesus and the confidence a Christian can have as a result. In Colossians 3, he spells out the implications this must have for everyday living. Because we have been raised with Christ (v 1), we should raise our sights to where he is and where one day we will be. Then we will inevitably want to live in a way that reflects where we belong (in heaven, not in this world) and to whom we belong (Jesus Christ is our master—no one else is!).

4. **How is it possible to say that a Christian has already been raised with Christ? How can we know that this has happened?**
Paul deliberately blows our minds here! It is in the past tense because of what has already been achieved at the cross and resurrection. It is now as if there is a seat reserved in heaven for each person in Christ and marked with each person's name (v 3-4). Of course we cannot see this yet—but we trust in God's promises supremely because of his track-record in Christ.

5. **Find the expressions that talk about giving up the old way of life. What does each of them mean?**
   - "Put to death" (v 5) suggests that we must try to kill off our old way of thinking, which leads to ungodly living.
   - "Used to walk" (v 7) makes us think of our life as a way to be and about which we make choices each day—our daily walk.
   - "Rid yourselves" (v 8): like throwing out the old rubbish.
   - "Taken off" (v 9): like removing and discarding an old set of filthy clothes.

6. **Find the expressions that describe the way a believer should take up a new way of life. What extra motives for change does Paul mention here?**
"Put on the new self" (v 10): like clothing ourselves in new robes, that fit our new status as God's children (Galatians 3:27).
Our motivations should be driven by…
   - the coming just judgment of God (Colossians 3:6). He has made known what displeases him, so it is surely now our concern to live in such a way that we avoid that.
   - the fact that he has chosen us, that

he has demonstrated his love for us in undeserved and unimaginable ways, and that we are therefore forgiven completely (v 12-14).

7. **What do these phrases suggest that the change to living a new life will be like? What extra insight does verse 10 give into how this change takes place?**
Hard work! Growing in godliness will mean that we must struggle, fight and wrestle with our old nature. But the fight always starts with getting our head in the right place first! Understanding who we now are; the greatness of Jesus, who we are serving; and our ultimate destiny—the new creation. Verse 10 suggests the renewal that is taking place is God's work in us. As we work, God is also working to effect this change.

8. **What should a church actually look like, according to verses 11-14? Why?**
As members of God's people, we must treat one another as Christ has treated us. This means that a church that is seeking to follow their Lord will be filled with people growing in Christ-likeness, filled with truth and love, and with absolutely no partiality along racial or social lines—because in his choosing of people, God shows no such distinctions. Such a community is truly evangelistic!

9. **What makes setting "our hearts on things above" difficult? How can we encourage one another to keep a heavenly perspective?**
The heavenly world seems unreal because it is invisible. So a Christian needs constant reminders to see beyond the material and visible—reality is much bigger than what we see or feel! We need the Bible's reminders, but we also need the challenges of fellow believers who live lives that demonstrate a different set of values to others around us. Seeing someone resisting worldly ambitions or influences for the sake of Christ can make a profound impact—one reason for reading biographies of people who have done just that.

10. **How will these verses help you to resolve conflicts and disputes affecting the unity of your church or small group?**
Solving problems of disunity must start with ourselves—are there people we need to forgive or treat gently and kindly? We must avoid being quick to assume that divisions are other people's fault! Thinking like that could actually be part of the problem!
NOTE: Make sure that your group seeks to change their own lives, rather than push the blame elsewhere.

11. **What are the three essential ingredients for healthy life (v 15, 16, 17)?**
    - The peace of Christ (v 15): Our reconciliation to God through Christ (1:20) must lead to reconciliation with one another (compare 3:13).
    - The word of Christ (v 16): Without this, it would be practically

impossible to set our hearts on things above (v 1), such is the lure of the world. Notice how this word should permeate not just our teaching but also our singing.

- Gratitude to God (v 15, 17): This is no afterthought but is essential if we are to remember our dependence on God and what he has done for us. Once we are reminded of that, any sense of superiority over others is completely erased.

12. **Look through the "household code" in 3:18 – 4:1. How does the Christian attitude to relationships differ from modern views about personal rights?**
Each person is to be characterised by other-person-centredness. This will obviously look different for different people because we all have different roles within a home—that of the child is not the same as that of the parent! There are controversies here of course, but if we take the section as a whole, we can see how it subverts modern assumptions about personal rights. In that sense, the whole passage is countercultural today.
NOTE: Now will not be the time to go into submission and roles in marriage. Paul deals with this more extensively in Ephesians 5 – 6. If it will help to defuse a potential argument, note that in Paul's introduction to this question of headship and order in marriage, his first command in Ephesians 5:21 is that everyone should submit to everyone else out of reverence for Christ.

13. **What Paul says here was just as challengingly countercultural in the 1st century as it is now. What is the most important truth for slaves and masters to remember? How does this affect their relationship?**
The most vital relationship for both slave and master is the one each has with Jesus as Lord. That gives both individuals a heavenly perspective on how they relate to one another. Paul's instructions for the slave illustrate a vital truth about worship—the whole of life is about our dedication to and service of God (Colossians 3:23). It doesn't matter how menial or irrelevant a task might seem to us. Moreover, God's justice is perfect—something both slaves and masters (and in contemporary terms, employees and employers) need constantly to remember (3:25 – 4:1).

Pray

The Getting Personal section suggests that your group share a need in one of these relationship areas. Make sure you keep these needs confidential, and do what you can to follow up and support people in areas they are struggling in. Always try to bring your prayers back to the gospel motivation we should have to live a new life in Christ.

6

Jesus Our Ministry

Colossians 4:2-18

The Big Idea

When the gospel bears fruit in our lives, we will be dependent on God through prayer, actively seeking opportunities to proclaim the gospel to the world around, and working together and standing firm as a body of believers.

Summary

These final paragraphs are no afterthought. While they might at first seem to be a random collection of greetings and advice, there is a common thread. They all illustrate real life for those who trust the full revelation of God in Christ and the finished work of Christ on the cross. At the very least, they remind us that the Christian life is about living together as a community of believers. There is no escapism here, since, clearly, life has its struggles and problems (for example, Paul's imprisonment, 4:3; the implicit challenge of speaking to non-believers, v 4:5-6; and Paul's acknowledgment of the need for friends and colleagues, v 11).

Despite this, there is real confidence—confidence that praying to God makes a difference (v 2 and 12), and confidence that Christian ministry is, in essence, about serving the "kingdom of God" (v 11). Most significant in the light of the whole letter is the subject of Epaphras' prayer in verse 12: "that you may stand firm in all the will of God, mature and fully assured". It was precisely this assurance that the Colossian false teachers undermined; and it is precisely this assurance that Paul sought to bolster and stabilise by writing to the Colossian Christians.

Optional Extra

Consider doing some role-play in the group, as a way of helping people to be prepared for the difficult questions people commonly ask. Use this to sharpen one another up, especially in terms of aiding clarity in communicating gospel truths.

Guidance for Questions

1. **Who are the people who have influenced you most in your Christian walk? What aspects of their lives and ministry made them such an influence?**
   Make sure people keep their answers very concise so that everyone has a chance to give an answer (if they want to) without this question taking up the bulk of your time together!

2. **How do these verses give us guidance...**

- **in our prayer priorities?**
  "Being watchful" points to the need for dependence on God for both the opportunities and challenges of living in an unbelieving world. Being

"thankful" reminds us that, whatever our circumstances, there are always things to praise God for.

Paul asks for prayer for gospel opportunities, but also he prays for preaching clarity. This is a challenge and an encouragement. Paul needed it; so do we. But Paul also struggled to communicate the gospel—we should not think that our difficulties in articulating the gospel mean we should not be doing it! We must also pray for open doors and clarity of gospel preaching for those who are specifically called to the work of evangelism.

- **in our outreach?**
  Look for God to open a door. Be prepared to proclaim the gospel clearly. Be prepared to suffer for it. (Paul was "in chains".) Live a godly life and be "wise" towards outsiders (= think about how they think, so you can relate the gospel to them effectively). Be a good conversationalist.

  NOTE: If people are overwhelmed by the challenge to share the gospel with others, remind them that the verses here address plural people. In other words, the evangelistic effort is something that the church does as a whole, and so a variety of approaches and styles are valid. But clarity in communicating the gospel is essential for us all. If people need help in this, challenge them to learn a simple gospel outline such as *Two Ways to Live*.

3. **What is the significance of Paul's use of the expression "the mystery of Christ"? (Compare with 1:27.)**
   This is the profound privilege of the Christian—Gentile or Jew: knowing God in all his fullness in Christ. With false teachers on the prowl undermining this, no wonder Paul prays for clarity when he proclaims this. It suggests that the content of our message must be primarily about the person and work of our Lord Jesus Christ.

4. **Despite the costs involved, why can we be confident when we share the gospel with others?**
   God is the one who opens doors (4:3). God is the one whose message is being preached—he kept it secret until the right time to open up the "mystery of Christ" to the Gentile world (v 3); he gives the opportunities to proclaim it (v 5) and, by implication, is the one who provides answers to every question (v 6).

5. **What practical steps can we take to ensure that...**

- **we pray with these priorities?**
  It is helpful to keep prayer lists and prayer diaries, as well as to work systematically through the Bible, so that we are challenged by its wide scope. If we are not praying for open doors or gospel opportunities, it is not likely that we will either notice or make the most of them when they come.

- **we are proclaiming the mystery of Christ clearly?**
  As well as praying like this, we need

to work hard at our clarity. Learning a gospel outline can help us to explain the gospel clearly, as does being prepared for different questions. It is perfectly reasonable to be caught out once—but it is irresponsible if we have not made an attempt to find answers and are stumped by the same question twice.

- **we fill our conversation with the salt of grace?**
  Again prayer is the key—so that we are depending on God for what we say. But it also means being proactive and looking for those opportunities to speak grace—which means both being gracious and speaking of the gospel grace of God.

6. **What virtues do the individuals Paul mentions have in common?**
   Being part of the Christian family is a key theme: Tychicus is a dear brother (v 7) as is Onesimus (v 9). Yet most of the people are mentioned because of their faithfulness in gospel ministry, often at great personal cost: again Tychicus (v 7), Aristarchus (v 10), Mark and Jesus Justus (v 10-11), and Epaphras (v 12).

7. **What do we learn about the nature of and priorities for prayer from the description of Epaphras in verses 12-13?**
   Epaphras was persistent in prayer—Paul's word for "wrestling" described the intense wrestling matches in the ancient world. There are connotations of Jacob wrestling with God (Genesis 32:22-32)—yet here Epaphras was doing it on the Colossians' behalf. It points to the urgency of their concern in the face of these false teachers. (See Colossians 1:7; 1:29 – 2:1.)

8. **Why do you think Paul signs off with a reminder of his chains (v 18)?**
   It reminds them that the message he preached cost him a great deal—but that in Paul's mind it was still worth it, such is the wonder of the gospel of the Christ, who is fully God, dying to reconcile his universe. It is something therefore that the Colossians should also be prepared to suffer for.

Explore More

- ***Read verse 14 and 2 Timothy 4:10. What can we learn from the story of Demas?***
  The reference in 2 Timothy 4:10 is a sad reminder that even active believers who are close to great teaching, enjoying Christian fellowship, and in the thick of active Christian service are still vulnerable to falling away. Use this to remind your group that we need constantly to fight the holiness battles of chapter 3, or else the old self will reassert itself with potentially disastrous consequences.

---

9. **Paul's description of his friends focuses on their hard work and service for the gospel. How can we encourage one another to**

persevere in our service of the Lord, his people and those who do not yet know him?

We need one another—teamwork and gospel partnership are vital. Prayer triplets are a great help for this—perhaps with a couple of others from the same office or neighbourhood. It is also good to have a close friend to be accountable to, who has permission to ask us difficult questions about our personal walk and perseverance. Above all, we need to be part of a local Christian church, to serve and be served.

10. **How does the prayer of Epaphras (4:12) sum up the big message of the letter to the Colossians? Write a sentence summarising the main point Paul has been trying to convey to them.**

    "Stand firm": Paul's main aim in writing this letter is to ensure that believers stand firm on the only solid rock there is—a full understanding of who Jesus Christ is and what he has done for and in us.

    - "In all the will of God": A shallow grasp of the gospel will leave us open to false teaching, as it will create a dissatisfaction in our lives that others will seek to exploit.
    - "Mature and fully assured": By appreciating the greatness of Christ and the fullness we have in him.

11. **What advice (from Colossians) would you give the following people?**

    These will revise what people have learned in Colossians. Answers might include the following.

- **A timid young Christian who wants to be more confident as a believer.**
  This Christian needs to understand exactly who they are following. Jesus is the Creator and Lord of all creation, who has died and risen again for Christians. We are already secure and safe in heaven with him.

- **Someone who claims to have discovered "something new" in the Christian life.**
  You will need to question this believer. If it is something that tries to add to or subtract from the work of Christ, then they need to know it is wrong. If it is a "technique" they have discovered, they need to understand that it will have no power to change their hearts and lives. Only by sticking to the gospel and growing in an appreciation of it will they be truly changed and brought to maturity.

- **Someone who wants to know how to grow as a Christian.**
  To grow, we need to focus on Jesus and the gospel. Perhaps suggest they work at the three marks of 3:15-17. Let Christ's peace (i.e. the gospel that has saved you) be the motivation for growing in godliness and relating to others. The word of Christ should be growing in you, as you read and study Scripture to know God and his will better. And a growing thankfulness to God for all things is a mark of maturity.

7

Jesus Our Unity

Philemon v 1-25

The Big Idea

Christ's gospel must not just be theoretical—it is supposed to transform our relationships. But this is sometimes easier said than done.

Summary

Paul's letter to Philemon gives us a striking example of a challenge to someone's discipleship. Is the grace and peace that Paul talked about in Colossians really realistic and workable? Is Philemon willing to be reconciled to a fellow believer even though that feels very hard?

Philemon was evidently one of the few Colossian Christians that Paul knew personally. It's apparent in verses 1-7 that he is a much-loved member of the church and a model of love shown without favouritism or discrimination. Philemon shows his faith by his deeds. But this faith is about to be tested.

In verse 8 Paul gets to the point of his letter: an appeal on behalf of someone called Onesimus. We find out that Onesimus is a slave belonging to Philemon (v 16). He ran away and took refuge with Paul—and has now become a Christian. Now Onesimus is returning to Philemon, and Paul urges Philemon to show him love.

The strength of Paul's relationships with both Philemon and Onesimus is plain. Philemon is Paul's beloved fellow worker (v 1) while Onesimus is his "son" (v 10). Paul wishes to see the same love displayed between Philemon and Onesimus, encouraging Philemon to view his former slave as a dear brother in Christ (v 16). In his culture, Philemon would seem to have every right to punish Onesimus severely, but Paul asks for the opposite: a complete reconciliation, in which Onesimus will be treated just as Paul himself would be.

We don't know what happened in the end. But this letter is a demonstration of how the grace of Jesus can transform our relationships. It challenges us to love each other deeply and be reconciled to one another. This is not easy, but it is vital as we seek to clothe ourselves with the "new self" that we have been gifted in Christ (Colossians 3:9-10).

Optional Extra

Play some simple games in which teamwork is required—this might be a family board game or something more active like a three-legged race. After you have explained the game, handicap one member of each team in some way (perhaps by blindfolding them). The point is to demonstrate that working together in unity is sometimes more difficult than it seems in theory!

Guidance for Questions

1. **When is it especially challenging to live with peace and grace towards each other?**

   Examples might include...

   - when you are overworked or overtired and struggling to be patient.
   - when someone is repeatedly sinning in the same way or has not said sorry for a wrong they have done.
   - when people come from very different backgrounds or have very different personalities and so find it difficult to understand each other.
   - when family conflict or historic trauma are part of the mix.

   It probably isn't a good idea to let this discussion become too specific or too deep—the point is simply to acknowledge that while being reconciled to each other may sound good in theory, it isn't always easy to put into practice.

2. **According to verses 4-7, how is Philemon already putting his faith into action?**

   He shows love for "all" God's people (v 4)—a love that refreshes their hearts (v 7). (This might sound a little limp, but it's a phrase with military origins, describing the recuperation an army might need after being exhausted by a forced march.) Philemon is in "partnership" with Paul; they have a deep bond that stems from their common bond with Christ.

   - **Where does Paul see room for growth?**

     In verse 6 Paul prays that Philemon's understanding will deepen.

3. **We can see this as a real-life example of Colossians 1:10 and 3:10. How so?**

   Both these verses from Colossians point to a continuing renewal or growth in a Christian. The Christian life is never static. Philemon's faith is not in doubt, but he still needs to deepen his understanding and grow in his knowledge of Jesus.

4. **Write down what we have learned about Paul, Philemon and Onesimus by the end of verse 12.**

- **Paul**
  - He is "a prisoner of Christ Jesus"—in prison because of his gospel ministry (v 1, 9).
  - He is an old man (v 9).
  - He is prayerful and thankful (v 4, 6).
  - He feels great affection towards Philemon, Onesimus and many other believers.
  - He is sending Onesimus "back to" Philemon.

- **Philemon**
  - He is a dear friend and fellow worker of Paul (v 1).
  - A church meets in his home (v 2).
  - He is faithful and loving (v 4-7).

- **Onesimus**
  - Paul regards him as his "son" (v 10).
  - He is useful to Paul (v 11).
  - He is being sent "back to" Philemon (v 12)—so he must have been with Philemon previously.

5. Before we move on to what Paul wants Philemon to do, look again at verses 1-12 and consider how Paul talks about these two friends. What are they to him? And why (as far as we can tell)?

Paul feels towards these two believers with the affection of Christ Jesus. He speaks of Philemon as his brother (v 7) and of Onesimus as his son (v 10). This is how deeply he cares about them! Why? Because of Jesus. These men have experienced the reconciliation and unity that can only come through being fellow recipients of the gospel of grace.

6. Reflect on the relationships in your own church. How similar or different are they to Paul's relationships? Use the following questions to help you.

- **In what ways are people being partners in the faith (v 6)?**
- **How is that partnership deepening people's understanding or knowledge?**
- **How are people refreshing each other's hearts (v 7)?**
- **Do you speak to each other on the basis of love (v 9)—Christ's love, which reconciles us to God and to each other? Are there any relationships that have more to do with authority or power than love?**
- **Are people treating each other as spiritual family members (v 10)? What does that look like in the modern Western world?**

Serving God's kingdom is about relationships—it is people. It can be surprisingly easy to lose sight of this. These questions are designed to help you celebrate the ways in which you are loving each other as a church, and to discern the ways in which you are falling short. Be careful not to let the discussion become one of complaining and finding fault—if you think this will be tempting for the group, it may be better to stick to the positive parts of each question and avoid the negative parts.

And remember, we love because Christ first loved us—so you may wish to close your discussion with prayer, asking God to speak to your hearts, deepen your understanding, and work in you to make you more like Jesus.

7. So why is Paul sending Onesimus back to Philemon? What is he hoping Philemon will do?

Paul is asking Philemon to welcome Onesimus as a brother (v 16, 17). He also suggests that Philemon might do "even more than I ask" (v 21), which may be a hint at the possibility of giving Onesimus his freedom.

8. What reasons does Paul give Philemon for this? Think about...

- **the changes in Onesimus (v 11, 16).**
  Onesimus has become more useful (v 11), but more importantly his identity has changed; he is now a brother in Christ (v 16).
- **God's plan (v 15-16).**
  Paul suggests that Onesimus' flight

from Philemon could actually have been God's sovereign plan to bring Onesimus to Christ. Onesimus has been disobedient, but God can bring good out of human disobedience.

- **financial considerations (v 18).**
  It's possible that Onesimus stole money from Philemon when he ran away. But Paul doesn't want to let this be a source of conflict between them—he will pay any debts himself.
- **Philemon's relationship with Paul (v 17, 19-20).**
  Philemon owes Paul his very self (v 19)—he was converted through Paul's ministry. No financial loss can compare with that! So, Paul urges Philemon to treat Onesimus as he would treat Paul himself. Philemon owes Paul love, and by loving Onesimus, he will be refreshing Paul's heart (v 20).

Explore More

- ***Imagine yourself in the shoes of a slave owner in the 1st century. How would you have responded to Paul's words in Colossians 3:11 and Philemon v 15-16?***
  First-century slavery was not restricted to particular races, nor was it necessarily permanent. The fortunate few might have been able to buy their freedom. But while people were enslaved, their owners saw them as belonging to a different category. They had no moral problem with slavery, since it had been the "natural" way of things since the dawn of time. Paul's words would have been hard to hear, and considered scandalous and perhaps nonsensical. A world without slavery was simply unimaginable.
- ***What about if you were a slave—how would you have responded then?***
  You probably wouldn't have been able to believe your ears! You would be used to being invisible and ignored. It would be astonishing to hear yourself described as Paul describes Onesimus.
- ***Now imagine you are Paul, explaining to a slave owner and a slave why they are actually equals in Christ. What would you say? Base your answer on the Bible.***
  All have sinned (Romans 3:23), and so none of us deserve God's love. No person is better than another; no group of people is better than another. All of us need to be reconciled to God through Christ (Colossians 1:22); and in Christ, all of us become part of God's chosen people (Colossians 3:12). We are equally loved and of equal importance.

---

9. **How does all of this illustrate what Paul taught in Colossians 3:11-15? Draw out specific links.**
   - There is no difference in identity between free Christians and enslaved Christians (Colossians 3:11). In Philemon, Paul loves Philemon

and Onesimus similarly; he describes Onesimus as playing the same role that Philemon played; he wants Philemon to treat Onesimus as he would Paul. It all illustrates the idea that "Christ is all, and is in all".

- Paul describes God's people as "dearly loved" (Colossians 3:12). He speaks with a similar affectionate tone in Philemon.
- Paul encourages Philemon to treat Onesimus with the kindness, patience and forgiveness that he has described in Colossians 3:12-14.
- All in all, Paul's message to Philemon is one of peace between the believers, as in Colossians 3:15.

10. Paul closes with a message of grace (Philemon v 25). How have we seen him exemplify and encourage the grace (undeserved love) of Jesus in this letter?

Onesimus did not deserve reconciliation; he had wronged his master. Meanwhile, Philemon did not deserve Paul's paying off the losses that Onesimus had incurred. But Paul was able to look past the mistakes and sins of both men and show them real love.

11. What might be our blind spots today—aspects of modern life that we assume are normal and acceptable, despite challenges from the gospel? In particular, in what ways does Jesus' radical message of reconciliation impact us?

- Our society reinforces many divisions along ethnic and economic lines which then get mirrored in our churches. Even churches meeting in the same neighbourhood and sharing similar beliefs have little to do with each other because they reflect the surrounding social division.
- Western society encourages us to pursue wealth and security—many of us take it for granted that we should be saving to buy a house or investing money for our children's education. This may result in wealthier Christians missing opportunities to care for less well-off believers or churches.
- Our culture gives a picture of family relationships that often differs from the biblical one. Consider how we should treat the elderly; how men and women should work together in marriage; what values and priorities we should instil in our children; how we should relate to those who are single.

- **In those areas of life, how can we cultivate the kind of love, grace and peace that Paul shows in his letter to Philemon?**

You might like to choose two or three situations and try to imagine what the love shown by Paul would look like in those relationships.

The ability to show love, grace and peace comes from our view of Christ, our view of ourselves and our view of one another. We need to see ourselves and our fellow believers as Christ sees us: as sinners who have been gloriously redeemed. Only when we have a true view of this status before God will we be motivated to treat each other with radical love and grace.

12. **What is the one thing you most want to remember from your study of Colossians and Philemon?**
    It may be helpful to give group members time to flick back through this book to remind themselves of what you have seen.

God's Word For You

Accessible Commentaries That Everyone Can Enjoy

Old Testament, including:

New Testament, including:

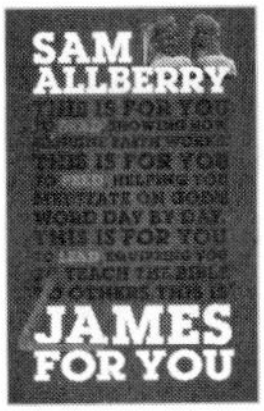

Less academic than a traditional commentary, these expository guides take you verse by verse through books of the Bible in an accessible, applied way. These flexible resources can enrich your personal devotions, help you lead small-group studies, or aid your sermon preparations.

Use with accompanying Good Book Guides to study these books of the Bible in small groups.

thegoodbook.com/for-you
thegoodbook.co.uk/for-you
thegoodbook.com.au/for-you

thegoodbook COMPANY

BIBLICAL | RELEVANT | ACCESSIBLE

At The Good Book Company we are dedicated to helping Christians and local churches grow. We believe that God's growth process always starts with hearing clearly what he has said to us through his timeless and flawless word—the Bible.

Ever since we opened our doors in 1991, we have been striving to produce resources that are biblical, relevant, and accessible. By God's grace, we have grown to become an international publisher, encouraging ordinary Christians of every age and stage and every background and denomination to live for Christ day by day and equipping churches to grow in their knowledge of God, their love for one another, and the effectiveness of their outreach.

Call one of our friendly team for a discussion of your needs or visit one of our local websites for more information on the resources and services we provide.

Your friends at The Good Book Company

thegoodbook.com | thegoodbook.co.uk
thegoodbook.com.au | thegoodbook.co.nz